LEARN YOUR NUMBERS THE SWiFTiE STYLE!

1 TO 20 with TAYLOR SWIFT

HANNAH KURRY

1

is for
the One
and Only

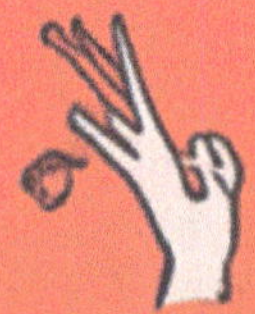

TAYLOR

2 IS FOR TWO GRAMMYS IN ONE NIGHT

CATS
TAYLOR
LVES
TO HUG

4

is
four
albums
re-recorded
and
loved by all.

5 IS FOR FIVE SECRET MESSAGES IN HER SONG LYRICS

is for
SIX
guitar
strings
Taylor
strums
in her
songs

7

is for
seven eras
in Taylor's
journey

8

is for EIGHT SCARVES

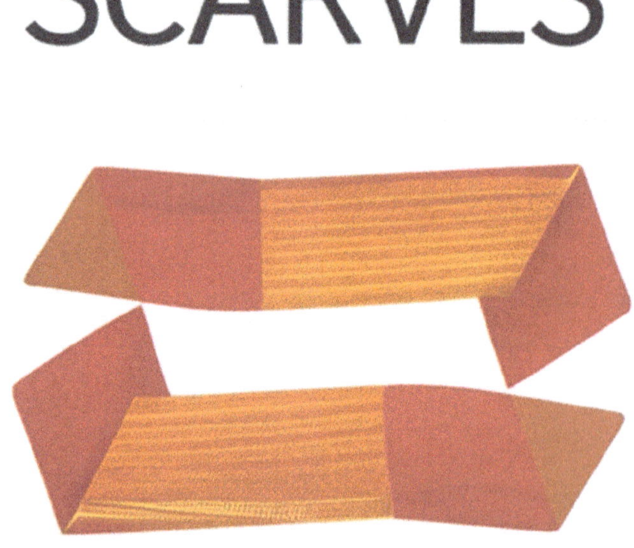

“RED”

forever iconic.

9

is for nine
enchanted awards
she won in
a single night.

Voolc
hoord

10

10 is for ten sparkling outfits
for a dazzling stage.

11

is for eleven hit singles on “1989”

12

is for twelve hours
to midnight

12
1
2
3
4
5
6
7
8
9
10
11

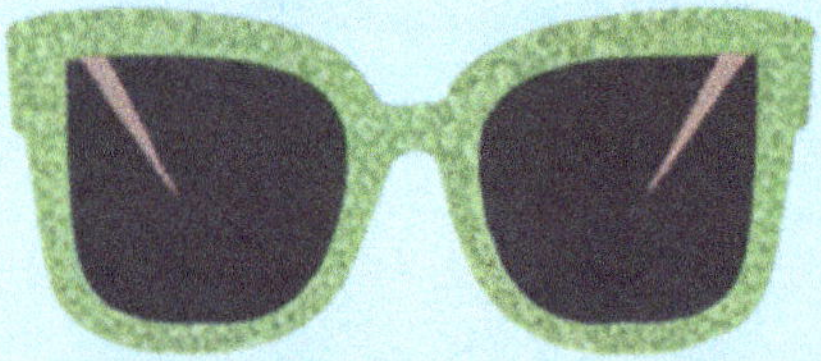

13

is for Taylor's
lucky number

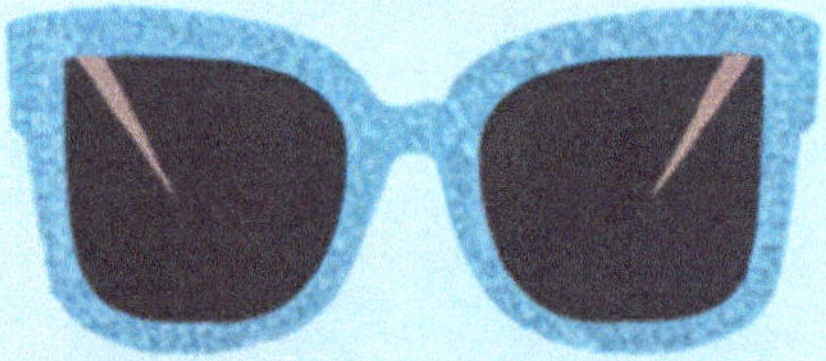

is for fourteen
friendship bracelets from fans.

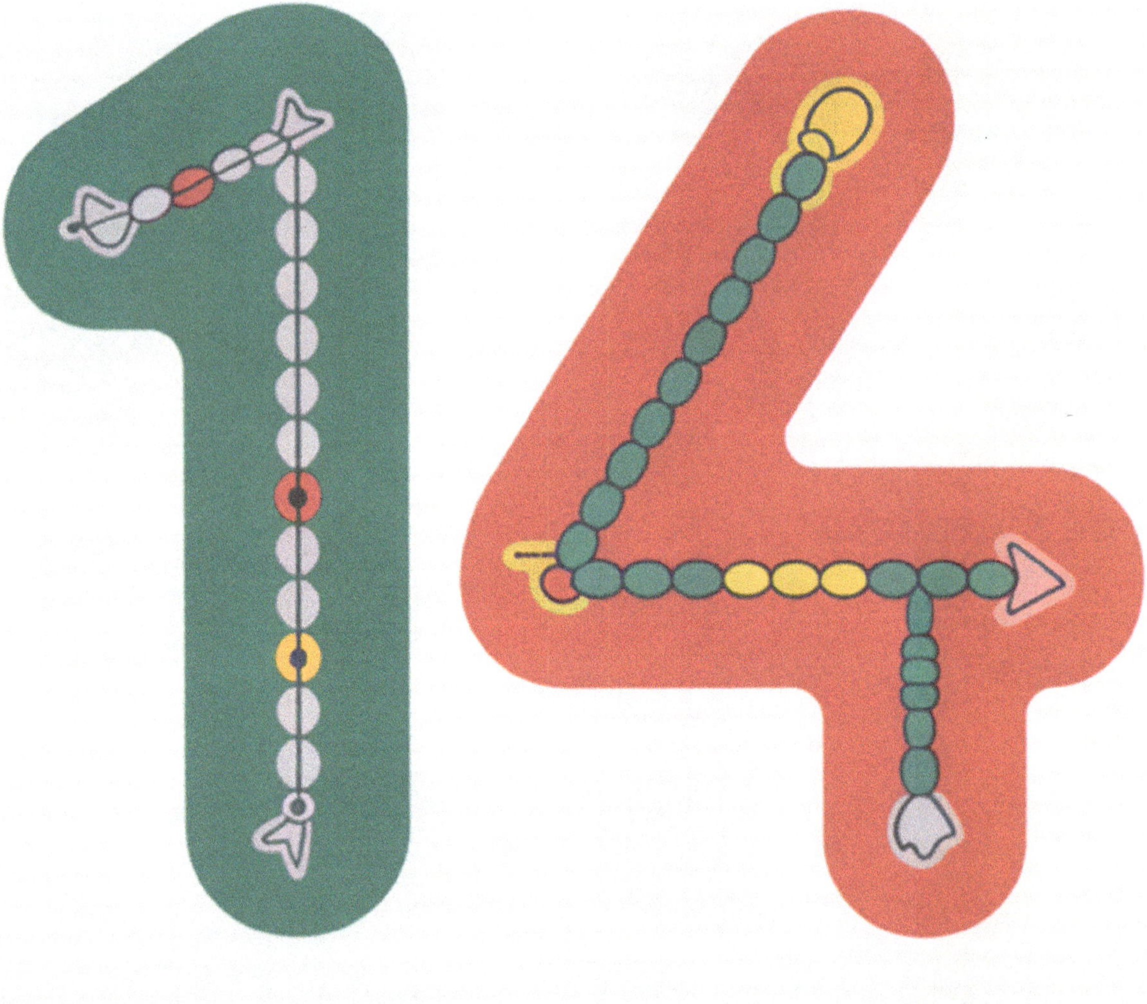

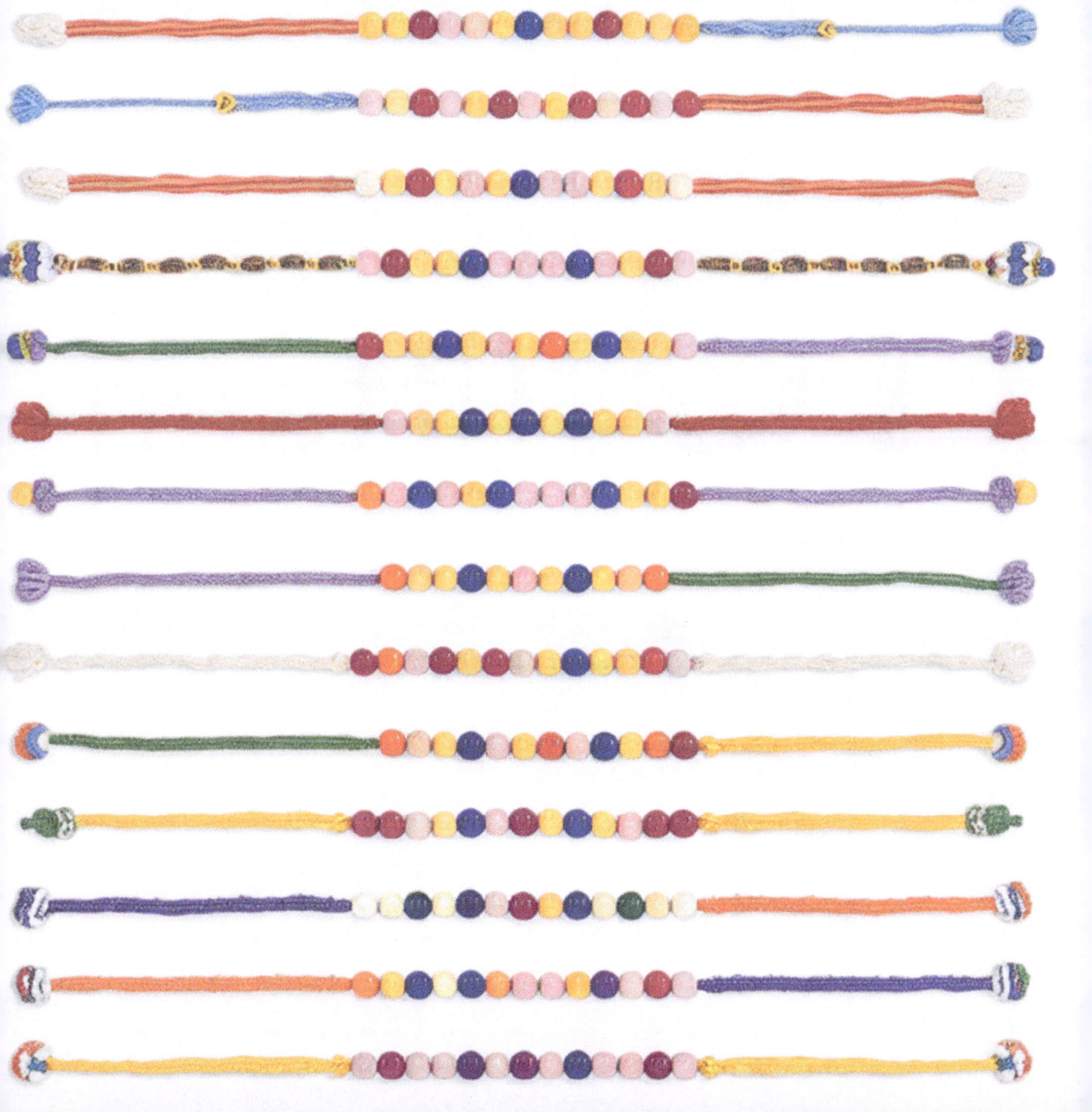

15 is for fifteen

polaroid pictures

16

is for sixteen
glittering hats
she's worn on stage

17

is for

seventeen pairs of
sparkling high heels

18

is for eighteen vinyl records in her collection.

19

is for nineteen colorful microphones she's sung with.

20

is for twenty golden picks played with.

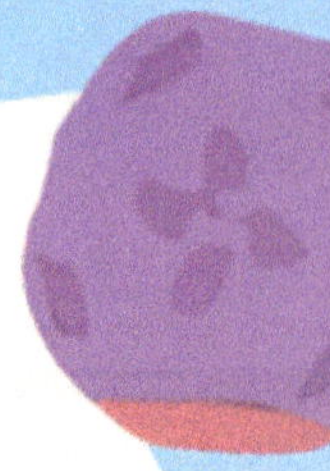

0 0 0 0 0
7 7 0 0 0
0 0 0 0 0
0 0 0 0 0